Jabez Lamar Monroe Curry

Education of the Negroes since 1860

Volume III

Jabez Lamar Monroe Curry

Education of the Negroes since 1860
Volume III

ISBN/EAN: 9783744735209

Printed in Europe, USA, Canada, Australia, Japan

Cover: Foto ©Thomas Meinert / pixelio.de

More available books at **www.hansebooks.com**

THE TRUSTEES OF THE JOHN F. SLATER FUND

OCCASIONAL PAPERS, No. 3

EDUCATION OF THE NEGROES

SINCE 1860

BY

J. L. M. CURRY, LL. D.

Secretary of the Trustees of the John F. Slater Fund

BALTIMORE

PUBLISHED BY THE TRUSTEES

1894

ANNOUNCEMENT.

The Trustees of the John F. Slater Fund propose to publish from time to time papers that relate to the education of the colored race. These papers are designed to furnish information to those who are concerned in the administration of schools, and also to those who by their official stations are called upon to act or to advise in respect to the care of such institutions.

The Trustees believe that the experimental period in the education of the blacks is drawing to a close. Certain principles that were doubted thirty years ago now appear to be generally recognized as sound. In the next thirty years better systems will undoubtedly prevail, and the aid of the separate States is likely to be more and more freely bestowed. There will also be abundant room for continued generosity on the part of individuals and associations. It is to encourage and assist the workers and the thinkers that these papers will be published.

Each paper, excepting the first number (made up chiefly of official documents), will be the utterance of the writer whose name is attached to it, the Trustees disclaiming in advance all responsibility for the statement of facts and opinions.

EDUCATION OF THE NEGROES
SINCE 1860.

INTRODUCTION.

The purpose of this paper is to put into permanent form a narrative of what has been done at the South for the education of the negro since 1860. The historical and statistical details may seem dry and uninteresting, but we can understand the significance of this unprecedented educational movement only by a study of its beginnings and of the difficulties which had to be overcome. The present generation, near as it is to the genesis of the work, cannot appreciate its magnitude, nor the greatness of the victory which has been achieved, without a knowledge of the facts which this recital gives in connected order. The knowledge is needful, also, for a comprehension of the future possible scope and kind of education to be given to the Afro-American race. In the field of education we shall be unwise not to reckon with such forces as custom, physical constitution, heredity, racial characteristics and possibilities, and not to remember that these and other causes may determine the limitations under which we must act. The education of this people has a far-reaching and complicated connection with their destiny, with our institutions, and possibly with the Dark Continent, which may assume an importance akin, if not superior, to what it had centuries ago. The partition of its territory, the international questions which are springing up, and the effect of contact with and government by a superior race, must necessarily give an enhanced importance to Africa as a factor in commerce, in relations of governments, and in civilization. England will soon have an unbroken line of territorial possessions from

Egypt to the Cape of Good Hope. Germany, France, Portugal, Italy, Spain, possibly Russia, will soon have such footholds in Africa as, whatever else may occur, will tend to the development of century-paralyzed resources.

What other superior races have done, and are doing, for the government and uplifting of the inferior races, which, from treaty or conquest, have been placed under their responsible jurisdiction, may help in the solution of our problem. Italy had a grand question in its unification ; Prussia a graver one in the nationalization of Germany, taxing the statesmanship of Stein, Bismarck, and their co-laborers ; Great Britain, in the administration of her large and widely remote colonial dependencies with their different races ; but our problem has peculiar difficulties which have not confronted other governments, and therefore demands the best powers of philanthropist, sociologist, and statesman.

The emergence of a nation from barbarism to a general diffusion of intelligence and property, to health in the social and civil relations ; the development of an inferior race into a high degree of enlightenment ; the overthrow of customs and institutions which, however indefensible, have their seat in tradition and a course of long observance ; the working out satisfactorily of political, sociological, and ethical problems— are all necessarily slow, requiring patient and intelligent study of the teachings of history and the careful application of something more than mere empirical methods. Civilization, freedom, a pure religion, are not the speedy outcome of revolutions and cataclysms any more than has been the structure of the earth. They are the slow evolution of orderly and creative causes, the result of law and preordained principles.

The educational work described in this paper has been most valuable, but it has been so far necessarily tentative and local. It has lacked broad and definite generalization, and, in all its phases, comprehensive, philosophical consideration. As auxiliary to a thorough study and ultimate better plans, the Slater Fund, from time to time, will have prepared and published papers bearing on different phases of the negro question.

I. The history of the negro on this continent is full of pathetic and tragic romance, and of startling, unparalleled incident. The seizure in Africa, the forcible abduction and cruel exportation, the coercive enslavement, the subjection to environments which emasculate a race of all noble aspirations and doom inevitably to hopeless ignorance and inferiority, living in the midst of enlightenments and noblest civilization and yet forbidden to enjoy the benefits of which others were partakers, for four years amid battle and yet, for the most part, having no personal share in the conflict, by statute and organic law and law of nations held in fetters and inequality, and then, in the twinkling of an eye, lifted from bondage to freedom, from slavery to citizenship, from dependence on others and guardianship to suffrage and eligibility to office— can be predicated of no other race. Other peoples, after long and weary years of discipline and struggle, against heaviest odds, have won liberty and free government. This race, almost without lifting a hand, unappreciative of the boon except in the lowest aspects of it, and unprepared for privileges and responsibilities, has been lifted to a plane of citizenship and freedom, such as is enjoyed, in an equal degree, by no people in the world outside of the United States.

Common schools in all governments have been a slow growth, reluctantly conceded, grudgingly supported, and perfected after many experiments and failures and with heavy pecuniary cost. Within a few years after emancipation, free and universal education has been provided for the negro, without cost to himself, and chiefly by the self-imposed taxes of those who, a few years before, claimed his labor and time without direct wage or pecuniary compensation.

II. Slavery, recognized by the then international law and the connivance and patronage of European sovereigns, existed in all the colonies prior to the Declaration of Independence, and was reinforced by importation of negroes from Africa

in foreign and New England and New York vessels.   In
course of time it was confined to the Southern States, and
the negroes increased in numbers at a more rapid rate than
did the whites, even after the slave trade was abolished and
declared piracy.

For a long time there was no general exclusion by law of
the slaves from the privileges of education.   The first pro-
hibitory and punitive laws were directed against unlawful
assemblages of negroes, and subsequently of free negroes and
mulattoes, as their influence in exciting discontent or insurrection was deprecated and guarded against.   Afterwards,
legislation became more general in the South, prohibiting
meetings for teaching reading and writing.   The Nat Turner
insurrection in Southampton County, Virginia, in 1831,
awakened the Southern States to a consciousness of the perils,
which might environ or destroy them, from combinations of
excited, inflamed, and ill-advised negroes.

As documents and newspapers tending to inflame discontent
and insurrection were supposed to have been the immediate
provocation to this conspiracy for murder of whites and for
freedom of the blacks, laws were passed against publishing
and circulating such documents among the colored population, and strengthening the prohibitions and penalties against
education.

Severe and general as were these laws, they rarely applied,
and were seldom, if ever, enforced, against teaching of individuals or of groups on plantations, or at the homes of the
owners.   It was often true that the mistress of a household,
or her children, would teach the house servants, and on Sun-
days include a larger number.   There were also Sunday
Schools in which black children were taught to read, notably
the school in which Stonewall Jackson was a leader.   It is
pleasant to find recorded in the memoir of Dr. Boyce, a
Trustee of this Fund from its origin until his death, that, as
an editor, a preacher, and a citizen, he was deeply interested
in the moral and religious instruction of the negroes.

After a most liberal estimate for the efforts made to teach the negroes, still the fact exists that, as a people, they were wholly uneducated in schools. Slavery doomed the millions to ignorance, and in this condition they were when the war began.

III. Almost synchronously with the earliest occupation of any portion of the seceding States by the Union Army, efforts were begun to give the negroes some schooling. In September, 1861, under the guns of Fortress Monroe, a school was opened for the "contrabands of war." In 1862, schools were extended to Washington, Portsmouth, Norfolk, and Newport News, and afterwards to the Port Royal islands on the coast of South Carolina, to Newbern and Roanoke Island in North Carolina. The proclamation of emancipation, January 1, 1863, gave freedom to all slaves reached by the armies, increased the refugees, and awakened a fervor of religious and philanthropic enthusiasm for meeting the physical, moral, and intellectual wants of those suddenly thrown upon charity. In October, 1863, General Banks, then commanding the Department of the Gulf, created commissioners of enrollment, who established the first public schools for Louisiana. Seven were soon in operation, with twenty-three teachers and an average attendance of 1422 scholars. On March 22, 1864, he issued General Order, No. 38, which constituted a Board of Education " for the rudimental instruction of the freedmen " in the Department, so as to " place within their reach the elements of knowledge."

The Board was ordered to establish common schools, to employ teachers, to acquire school sites, to erect school buildings where no proper or available ones for school purposes existed, to purchase and provide necessary books, stationery, apparatus, and a well selected library, to regulate the course of studies, and " to have the authority and perform the same duties that assessors, supervisors, and trustees had in the Northern States in the matter of establishing and conducting common schools." For the performance of the duties enjoined, the Board was empowered to "assess and levy a school tax upon real and personal property, including crops of plantations." These taxes were to be sufficient to defray expense and cost of establishing, furnishing, and conducting the schools for the period of one year. When the tax list and schedules should be placed in the hands of the Parish Provost Marshal, he was to collect and pay over within thirty days to the School Board. Schools previously established were transferred to this Board; others were opened, and in December, 1864, they reported under their supervision 95 schools, 162 teachers, and 9,571 scholars. This system continued until December, 1865, when the power to levy the tax was suspended. An official report of later date says: " In this sad juncture the freedmen expressed a willingness to endure and even petitioned for increased taxation in order that means for supporting their schools might be obtained."

On December 17, 1862, Col. John Eaton was ordered by General Grant to assume a general supervision of freedmen in the Department of Tennessee and Arkansas. In the early autumn of that year schools had been established, and they were multiplied during 1863 and 1864. In the absence of responsibility and supervision there grew up abuses and complaints. By some "parties engaged in the work" of education, "exorbitant charges were made for tuition," and agents and teachers, "instead of making common cause for the good of those they came to benefit, set about detracting, perplexing, and vexing each other." " Parties and conflicts had arisen." " Frauds had appeared in not a few instances—evil minded, irresponsible, or incompetent persons imposing upon those not prepared to defeat or check them." " Bad faith to fair promises had deprived the colored people of their just dues."[1]

On September 26, 1864, the Secretary of War, through Adjutant General Thomas, issued Order No. 28, in which he said: "To prevent confusion and embarrassment, the General

[1] See report of Chaplain Warren, 1864, relating to colored schools.

Superintendent of Freedmen will designate officers, subject to his orders, as Superintendents of colored schools, through whom he will arrange the location of all schools, teachers, occupation of houses, and other details pertaining to the education of the freedmen." In accordance with this order, Col. Eaton removed his headquarters from Vicksburg to Memphis. On October 20, 1864, he issued sixteen rules and regulations for the guidance of superintendents and teachers of colored schools in his supervision. These instructions to subordinates were wise and provided for the opening of a sufficient number of schools, for the payment of tuition fees from 25 cents to $1.25 per month for each scholar, according to the ability of the parents; for the admission free of those who could not pay and the furnishing of clothing by the aid of industrial schools, for the government of teachers in connection with the societies needing them, &c. The "industrial schools" were schools in which sewing was taught, and in which a large quantity of the clothing and material sent from the North was made over or made up for freedmen's use, and were highly "useful in promoting industrious habits and in teaching useful arts of housewifery." The supervision under such a competent head caused great improvement in the work, but department efforts were hindered by some representatives of the benevolent societies who did not heartily welcome the more orderly military supervision. An Assistant Superintendent, March 31, 1865, reports, in and around Vicksburg and Natchez, 30 schools, 60 teachers, and 4,393 pupils enrolled; in Memphis, 1,590 pupils, and in the entire supervision, 7,360 in attendance.

General Eaton submitted a report of his laborious work which is full of valuable information. Naturally, some abatement must be made from conclusions which were based on the wild statements of excited freedmen, or the false statements of interested persons. "Instinct of unlettered reason" caused a hegira of the blacks to camps of the Union Army, or within protected territory. The "negro population floated or was

kicked about at will." Strict supervision became urgent to
secure " contraband information " and service, and protect the
ignorant, deluded people from unscrupulous harpies. " Mental and moral enlightenment " was to be striven for, even in
those troublous times, and it was fortunate that so capable and
faithful an officer as General Eaton was in authority.

All the operations of the supervisors of schools did not give
satisfaction, for the Inspector of Schools in South Carolina
and Georgia, on October 13, 1865, says : " The Bureau does
not receive that aid from the Government and Government
officials it had a right to expect, and really from the course
of the military officials in this Department, you might think
that the only enemies to the Government are the agents of
the Bureau."

IV. By act of Congress of March 3, 1865, the Freedmen's
Bureau was created. The scope of its jurisdiction and work
extended far beyond education. It embraced abandoned lands
and the supply of the negroes with food and clothing, and during 1865 as many as 148,000 were reported as receiving rations.
The Quartermaster and Commissary Departments were placed
at the service of the agents of the Bureau, and, in addition to
freedom, largesses were lavishly given to " reach the great
and imperative necessities of the situation." Large and comprehensive powers and resources were placed in the hands of
the Bureau, and limitations of the authority of the Government were disregarded in order to meet the gravest problem of
the century. Millions of recently enslaved negroes, home-
less, penniless, ignorant, were to be saved from destitution or
perishing, to be prepared for the sudden boon of political
equality, to be made self-supporting citizens and to prevent
their freedom from becoming a curse to themselves and their
liberators. The Commissioner was authorized " to seize, hold,
use, lease, or sell all buildings and tenements and any lands
appertaining to the same, or otherwise formally held, under
color of title by the late Confederate States, and buildings or

lands held in trust for the same, and to use the same, or appropriate the proceeds derived therefrom, to the education of the freed people." He was empowered also to "coöperate with private benevolent associations in aid of the freedmen." The Bureau was attached to the War Department and was at first limited in duration to one year, but was afterwards prolonged. General O. O. Howard was appointed Commissioner, with assistants. He says he was invested with "almost unlimited authority" and that the act and orders gave "great scope and liberty of action." "Legislative, judicial, and executive powers were combined, reaching all the interests of the freedmen." On June 2, 1865, the President ordered all officers of the United States to turn over to the Bureau "all property, funds, lands, and records in any way connected with freedmen and refugees." This bestowment of despotic power was not considered unwise because of the peculiar exigencies of the times and the condition of the freedmen, who, being suddenly emancipated by a dynamic process, were without schools, or teachers, or means to procure them. To organize the work, a Superintendent of Schools was appointed for each State. Besides the regular appropriation by Congress, the Military authorities aided the Bureau. Transportation was furnished to teachers, books, and school furniture, and material aid was given to all engaged in education.

General Howard used his large powers to get into his custody the funds scattered in the hands of many officers, which could be made available for the freedmen. Funds bearing different names were contributed to the work of "colored education."[1] During the war some of the States sent money, to officers serving in the South, to buy substitutes from among the colored people to fill up their quota under the draft. A portion of the bounty money thus sent, by an order of Gen. B. F. Butler, August 4, 1864, was retained in the hands of officers who had been superin-

[1] See Spec. Ed. Rep., District of Columbia, p. 259.

tendents of negro affairs, and by the President's order of June 2, 1865 was turned over to the disbursing officers of the Bureau of Freedmen. After the organization of the Bureau, Gen. Howard instructed agents to turn money, held by them, over to the chief disbursing officer of the Bureau. This was in no sense public money, but belonged to individuals, enlisted as contraband recruits to fill the State quotas. What was unclaimed of what was held in trust under Gen. Butler's order was used for educational purposes.

In the early part of 1867, the accounting officers of the Treasury Department ascertained that numerous frauds were being perpetrated on colored claimants for bounties under acts of Congress. Advising with General Howard, the Treasury officials drew a bill, which Congress enacted into a law, devolving upon the Commissioner the payment of bounties to colored soldiers and sailors. This enlarged responsibility gave much labor to General Howard, in his already multifarious and difficult duties, and made more honorable the acquittal which he secured when an official investigation was subsequently ordered upon his administration of the affairs of the Bureau.

The Act of Congress of July 16, 1866, gave a local fund, which was expended in the district in which it accrued, and besides there were general appropriations for the support of the Bureau, which were, in part, available for schools.

Mr. Ingle, writing of school affairs in the District in 1867 and 1868, says:

"Great aid was given at this period by the Freedmen's Bureau, which, not limiting its assistance to schools for primary instruction, did much toward establishing Howard University, in which no distinction was made on account of race, color, or sex, though it had originally been intended for the education of negro men alone."

The monograph of Edward Ingle on "The Negro in the District of Columbia"—one of the valuable Johns Hopkins

University Studies—gives such a full and easily accessible account of the education of the negroes in the District, that it is needless to enlarge the pages of this paper by a repetition of what he has so satisfactorily done.

The Bureau found many schools in localities which had been within the lines of the Union armies, and these, with the others established by its agency, were placed under more systematic supervision. In some States, schools were carried on entirely by aid of the funds of the Bureau, but it had the coöperation and assistance of various religious and benevolent societies. On July 1, 1866, Mr. Alvord, Inspector of Schools and Finances, reported 975 schools in fifteen States and the District, 1,405 teachers, and 90,778 scholars. He mentioned as worthy of note a change of sentiment among better classes in regard to freedmen's schools, and that the schools were steadily gaining in numbers, attainments, and general influence. On January 17, 1867, General Howard reports to the Secretary of War $115,261.56 as used for schools, and the Quartermaster's Department as still rendering valuable help. Education "was carried on vigorously during the year," a better feeling prevailing, and 150,000 freedmen and children "occupied earnestly in the study of books." The taxes, which had been levied for schools in Louisiana, under the administration of T. W. Conway, had been discontinued, but $500,000 were asked for schools and asylums. In 1867, the Government appointed Generals Steedman and Fullerton as Inspectors, and from General Howard's vehement reply to their report—which the War Department declines to permit an inspection of—it appears that their criticisms were decidedly unfavorable. Civilians in the Bureau were now displaced by army officers. In July, 1869, Mr. Alvord mentions decided progress in educational returns, increasing thirst for knowledge, greater public favor, and the establishment of 39 training schools for teachers, with 3,377 pupils. Four months later, General Howard says "hostility to schools and teachers has in great measure ceased." He reported the cost of the Bureau at $13,029,816, and earnestly recommended "the national legislature" to establish a general system of free schools, " furnishing to all children of a suitable age such instruction in the rudiments of learning as would fit them to discharge intelligently the duties of free American citizens." Solicitor Whiting had previously recommended that the head of the Freedmen's Bureau should be a cabinet officer, but this was not granted, and the Bureau was finally discontinued—its affairs being transferred to the War Department by Act of Congress, June 10, 1872. It is apparent from the reports of Sprague, Assistant Commissioner in Florida, and of Alvord in 1867 and 1870, that the agents of the Bureau sometimes used their official position and influence for organizing the freedmen for party politics and to control elections. A full history of the Freedmen's Bureau would furnish an interesting chapter in negro education, but a report from Inspector Shriver on October 3, 1873, says the Department has "no means of verifying the amount of retained bounty fund;" and on December 4, 1873, the Department complains of "the incomplete and disordered condition of the records of the late Bureau." (See Ex. Doc. No. 10, 43d Con., 1st Ses., and Ho. Mis. Doc. No. 87, 42d Con., 3d Ses.)

That no injustice may be done to any one, the answer of the " Record and Pension Office, War Department," May 21, 1891, to my application for statistics drawn from the records, is embodied in this paper. So far as the writer has been able to investigate, no equally full and official account has heretofore been given.

———————

" The following consolidated statement, prepared from records of Superintendents of Education of the Bureau of Refugees, Freedmen, and Abandoned Lands, shows the number of schools, teachers, and pupils in each State, under control of said Bureau, and the amount expended for Schools, Asylums, construction and rental of school buildings, transportation of teachers, purchase of books, etc. :—

1865-1866.

Number of Schools	1,264
Number of Teachers	1,793
Number of Pupils	111,193
Amount Expended by Bureau	$ 225,722 94
Received from Freedmen	18,500 00
Received from Benevolent Associations	83,200 00

1867.

Number of Schools	1,673
Number of Teachers	2,032
Number of Pupils	108,245
Amount Expended	$ 115,330 00
From Freedmen	17,200 00
From Benevolent Associations	65,687 00

1868.

Number of Schools	1,759
Number of Teachers	2,104
Number of Pupils	102,562
Amount Expended	$ 903,210 20
From Freedmen	42,150 00
From Benevolent Associations	154,726 50

1869.

Number of Schools	1,942
Number of Teachers	2,472
Number of Pupils	108,185
Amount Expended	$ 591,267 56
From Freedmen	85,726 00
From Benevolent Associations	27,200 00

1870.

Number of Schools	1,900
Number of Teachers	2,376
Number of Pupils	108,135
Amount Expended	$ 480,737 82
From Freedmen	17,187 00
From Benevolent Associations	4,240 00

2

" This statement or statistical table is made up from the reports of the Superintendents of Education of the several States under the control of the Bureau from 1865 to 1870, when government aid to the freedmen's schools was withdrawn. It embraces the number of schools established or maintained, the number of teachers employed, the number of pupils, and the amount expended for school purposes in each State and the District of Columbia. The expenditures also include the amounts contributed by the Bureau for the construction and maintenance of asylums for the freedmen, which cannot be separated from the totals given.

" The table is based upon the reports of the School Superintendents, and has been prepared with great care. The results thus obtained, however, differ in some material respects from the figures given by the Commissioner of the Freedmen's Bureau in his annual reports. These discrepancies, which this Department is unable to reconcile or explain, will be seen by a comparison of the table with the following statement made from the reports of the Commissioner :

1866.

Number of Schools	975
Number of Teachers	1,405
Number of Pupils	90,778

Disbursements for School Purposes.

By the Bureau	$	123,659 39
By the Benevolent Associations		82,200 00
By the Freedmen		18,500 00
Total		$224,359 39

1867.

Number of Schools	1,839
Number of Teachers	2,087
Number of Pupils	111,442

Disbursements for School Purposes.

By the Bureau...$ 581,345 48
By the Benevolent Associations.................................. 65,087 01
By the Freedmen... 17,200 00
                                                                      ——————
    Total... $613,632 49

1868.

Number of Schools.. 1,831
Number of Teachers... 2,295
Number of Pupils.. 104,327

Disbursements for School Purposes.

By the Bureau..$ 965,896 67
By Benevolent Associations... 700,000 00
By the Freedmen [est'd]... 360,000 00
                                                                      ——————
    Total... $2,025,896 67

1869.

Number of Schools.. 2,118
Number of Teachers... 2,455
Number of Pupils... 114,522

Disbursements for School Purposes.

By the Bureau..$ 924,182 16
By Benevolent Associations... 365,000 00
By the Freedmen [est'd]... 190,000 00
                                                                      ——————
    Total... $1,479,182 16

1870.

Number of Schools.. 2,677
Number of Teachers... 3,300
Number of Pupils... 149,581

Disbursements for School Purposes.

By the Bureau..$ 976,853 29
By Benevolent Associations... 360,000 00
By the Freedmen [est'd]... 200,000 00
                                                                      ——————
    Total... $1,536,853 29

"It has been found impracticable to ascertain the amounts expended by the Freedmen's Bureau for Howard and Fisk Universities and the schools at Hampton, Atlanta, and New Orleans, the items of expenditure for these schools not being separated in the reports from the gross expenditures for school purposes."

A committee of investigation upon General Howard's use of the Bureau for his pecuniary aggrandizement were divided in opinion, but a large majority exonerated him from censure and commended him for the excellent performance of difficult duties. An equally strong and unanimous verdict of approval was rendered by a Court of Inquiry, General Sherman presiding, which was convened under an Act of Congress, February 13, 1874.

V. It has been stated that the Bureau was authorized to act in coöperation with benevolent or religious societies in the education of the negroes. A number of these organizations had done good service before the establishment of the Bureau and continued their work afterwards. The teachers earliest in the field were from the American Missionary Association, Western Freedmen's Aid Commission, American Baptist Home Mission Society, and the Society of Friends. After the surrender of Vicksburg and the occupation of Natchez, others were sent by the United Presbyterians, Reformed Presbyterians, United Brethren in Christ, Northwestern Freedmen's Aid Commission, and the National Freedmen's Aid Association. The first colored school in Vicksburg was started in 1863 by the United Brethren in the basement of a Methodist church.

The American Missionary Association was the chief body, apart from the Government, in the great enterprise of meeting the needs of the negroes. It did not relinquish its philanthropic work because army officers and the Federal Government were working along the same line. Up to 1866 its receipts were swollen by "the aid of the Free Will Baptists, the Wesleyans, the Congregationalists, and friends in Great Britain." From Great Britain it is estimated that "a million of dollars in money and clothing were contributed through various channels for the freedmen." The third decade of the Association, 1867–1876, was a marked era in its financial history. The Freedmen's Bureau turned over a large sum, which could be expended only in buildings. A congressional report says that between December, 1866, and May, 1870, the Association received $243,753.22. Since the Association took on a more distinctive and separate denominational character, because of the withdrawal of other denominations into organizations of their own, it, along with its church work, has prosecuted, with unabated energy and marked success, its educational work among the negroes. It has now under its control or support—

Chartered Institutions	6
Normal Schools	29
Common Schools	43

TOTALS.

Schools	78
Instructors	389
Pupils	12,609

PUPILS CLASSIFIED.

Theological	47
Collegiate	57
College Preparatory	192
Normal	1,091
Grammar	2,378
Intermediate	3,692
Primary	5,152

Some of these schools are not specially for negroes. It would be unjust not to give the Association much credit for Atlanta University and for Hampton Normal and Industrial Institute, which are not included in the above recapitulation,

as the latter stands easily first among all the institutions
designed for negro development, both for influence and use-
fulness.   During the war and for a time afterwards, the school
work of the Association was necessarily primary and transi-
tional, but it grew into larger proportions, with higher stand-
ards, and its normal and industrial work deserves special
mention and commendation.   From 1860 to October 1, 1893,
its expenditures in the South for freedmen, directly and indi-
rectly, including church extension as well as education, have
been $11,610,000.

VI. In 1866 was organized "The Freedmen's Aid and
Southern Society of the Methodist Episcopal Church." Under
that compact, powerful, well-disciplined, enthusiastic organization, more than $6,000,000 have been expended in the
work of education of negroes.   Dr. Hartzell said, before the
World's Congress in Chicago, that Wilberforce University, at
Xenia, Ohio, was established in 1857 as a college for colored
people, and "continues to be the chief educational centre of
African Methodism in the United States."   He reports, as
under various branches of Methodism, 65 institutions of learning for colored people, 388 teachers, 10,100 students,
$1,905,150 of property, and $652,500 of endowment.   Among
these is Meharry Medical College of high standard and excellent discipline, with dental and pharmaceutical departments
as well as medical.   Near 200 students have been gradu-
ated.   The School of Mechanic Arts in Central Tennessee
College, under the management of Professor Sedgwick, has a
fine outfit, and has turned out telescopes and other instru-
ments, which command a ready and remunerative market in
this and other countries.

VII. On April 16, 1862, slavery was abolished in the
District of Columbia.   By November, 13,000 refugees had
collected at Washington, Alexandria, Hampton, and Norfolk.

Under an unparalleled exigency, instant action was necessary. The lack of educational privileges led Christian societies to engage in educational work, at least in the rudiments of learning, for the benefit of these people, who were eager to be instructed. Even where education had not previously been a part of the functions of certain organizations, the imperative need of the liberated left no option as to duty. With the assistance of the Baptist Free Mission Society and of the Baptist Home Mission Society, schools were established in Alexandria as early as January 1, 1862, and were multiplied through succeeding years. After Appomatox, the Baptist Home Mission Society was formally and deliberately committed to the education of the blacks, giving itself largely to the training of teachers and preachers. In May, 1892, the Society had, under its management, 24 schools with 216 instructors, 4,861 pupils, of whom 1,756 were preparing to teach, school property worth $750,000 and endowment funds of $156,000. Probably, not less than 50,000 have attended the various schools. Since 1860, $2,451,859.65 have been expended for the benefit of the negroes. The Superintendent of Education says: " The aggregate amount appropriated for the salaries of teachers from the time the Society commenced its work until January, 1883, was:—District of Columbia, $59,243.57 ; Virginia, $65,254.44 ; North Carolina, $41,788.90; South Carolina, $29,683.71 ; Florida, $3,464.16 ; Georgia, $26,963.21 ; Alabama, $4,960.37 ; Mississippi, $6,611.05 ; Louisiana, $39,168.25 ; Texas, $2,272.18 ; Arkansas, $150 ; Tennessee, $57,898.86 ; Kentucky, $1,092.54 ; Missouri, $300. The following gives the aggregate amount appropriated for teachers and for all other purposes such as land, buildings, etc., from January, 1883, to January, 1893 :—District of Columbia, $103,110.01 ; Virginia, $193,974.08 ; North Carolina, $142,861.95 ; South Carolina, $137,157.79 ; Florida, $55,-923.96 ; Georgia, $314,061.48 ; Alabama, $35,405.86 ; Mississippi, $86,019.70 ; Louisiana, $33,720.93 ; Texas, $131,-225.27 ; Arkansas, $13,206.20 ; Tennessee, $164,514.05 ;

Kentucky, $49,798.56 ; Missouri, $6,543.13.   Until January, 1883, the appropriations for teachers and for lands, buildings, etc., were kept as separate items. I have already given the appropriations for the teachers up to that date. For grounds and buildings, $421,119.50 were appropriated." In connection with the Spelman Seminary and the Male School in Atlanta, there has been established, under intelligent and discriminating rules, a first class training department for teachers. A new commodious structure well adapted to the purpose, costing $55,000, was opened in December. At Spelman there is an admirable training school for nurses, where the pupils have hospital practice. Shaw University at Raleigh has the flourishing Leonard Medical School and a well equipped pharmacy.

VIII. The Presbyterian Church at the North, in May, 1865, adopted a deliverance in favor of special efforts in behalf of the "lately enslaved African race." From the 28th annual report of the Board of Missions for Freedmen, it appears that, besides building churches, special exertions have been put forth "in establishing parochial schools, in planting academies and seminaries, in equipping and supporting a large and growing university." The report mentions fifteen schools,—three in North Carolina, four in South Carolina, three in Arkansas, and one in each of the States of Texas, Mississippi, Virginia, Georgia, and Tennessee. $1,280,000 have been spent. "In the high schools and parochial schools, we have (May, 1893) 10,520 students who are being daily moulded under Presbyterian educational influence." The United Presbyterian Church reports for May, 1893, an enrollment in schools of 2,558. The Southern Presbyterians have a Theological Seminary in Birmingham, Alabama, which was first opened in Tuskaloosa in 1877.

IX. The Episcopal Church, through the Commission on Church Work among the Colored People, during the seven years of its existence, 1887–1893, has expended $272,068, but the expenditure is fairly apportioned between ministerial and teaching purposes. The schools are parochial " with an element of industrial training," and are located in Maryland, Virginia, North Carolina, Tennessee, and Alabama, but the " Reports " do not give the number of teachers and scholars. The Friends have some well conducted schools, notably the Schofield in Aiken, South Carolina. They have sustained over 100 schools and have spent $1,004,129. In the mission work of the Roman Catholic Church among the negroes, school work and church work are so blended that it has been very difficult to make a clear separation. Schools exist in Baltimore, Washington, and all the Southern States, but with how many teachers and pupils and at what cost the Report of the Commission for 1893 does not show. A few extracts are given. " We need," says one, " all the help possible to cope with the Public Schools of Washington. In fact our school facilities are poor, and, unless we can do something to invite children to our Catholic Schools, many of them will lose their faith." Another person writes : " Next year we shall have to exert all the influence in our power to hold our school. Within two doors of our school a large public school building is being erected ; this new public school building will draw pupils away from the Catholic School, unless the latter be made equally efficient in its work."

X. On February 6, 1867, George Peabody gave to certain gentlemen two million dollars in trust, to be used " for the promotion and encouragement of intellectual, moral, or industrial education among the young of the more destitute portions of the Southwestern States of our Union." This gift embraced both races, and Dr. Barnas Sears was fortunately selected as the General Agent, to whom was committed practically the administration of the Trust. In his first report he remarked that, in many of the cities aided by the Fund, provision was made for the children of both races, but said that, as the subject of making equal provision for the education of both races was occupying public attention, he thought it the safer and wiser course not to set up schools on a precarious foundation, but to confine help to public schools and make efforts in all suitable ways to improve or have established State systems of education. Still, in some localities aid was judiciously given, and the United States Superintendent of Education for the negroes in North Carolina gave testimony that but for the Peabody aid many of the colored schools would be closed. "Our Superintendents have aided largely in distributing the Peabody Fund in nearly all the States." "Great good has thereby been accomplished at very little added expense." The Peabody Fund bent its energies and directed its policy towards securing the establishment of State systems of education which should make adequate and permanent provision for universal education. State authorities would have more power and general influence than individuals, or denominational or private corporations. They represent the whole people, are held to a strict accountability, protect "from the charge of sectarianism and from the liability of being overreached by interested parties." State systems, besides, have a continuous life and are founded on the just principle that property is taxable for the maintenance of general education. The Fund now acts exclusively with State systems, and continues support to the negroes more efficiently through such agencies.

XI. Congress, by land grants since 1860, has furnished to the Southern States substantial aid in the work of Agricultural and Mechanical education. On March 2, 1867, the Bureau of Education was established for the collection and diffusion of information. This limited sphere of work has been so interpreted and cultivated that the Bureau, under its able Commissioners, especially under the leadership of that most accomplished American educator, Dr. W. T. Harris, has become one of the most efficient and intelligent educational

agencies on the continent. To the general survey of the
educational field and comparative exhibits of the position of
the United States and other enlightened countries, have been
added discussions by specialists, and papers on the various
phases of educational life, produced by the incorporation of
diverse races into our national life or citizenship. The Annual
Reports and Circulars of Information contain a vast mass of
facts and studies in reference to the colored people, and a digest
and collaboration of them would give the most complete history that could be prepared.

The Bureau and the Peabody Education Fund have been
most helpful allies in making suggestions in relation to legislation in school matters, and giving, in intelligible, practical
form, the experiences of other States, home and foreign, in
devising and perfecting educational systems. All the States
of the South, as soon as they recovered their governments, put
in operation systems of public schools which gave equal
opportunities and privileges to both races. It would be sin-
gularly unjust not to consider the difficulties, social, political,
and pecuniary, which embarrassed the South in the efforts to
inaugurate free education. It required unusual heroism to
adapt to the new conditions, but she was equal in fidelity and
energy to what was demanded for the reconstruction of society
and civil institutions. The complete enfranchisement of the
negroes and their new political relations, as the result of the
war and the new amendments to the Constitution, necessitated
an entire reorganization of the systems of public education.
To realize what has been accomplished is difficult, at best—
impossible, unless we estimate sufficiently the obstacles and
compare the facilities of to-day with the ignorance and bondage
of a generation ago, when some statutes made it an indictable
offence to teach a slave or free person of color. Comparisons
with densely populated sections are misleading, for in the
South the sparseness and poverty of the population are almost
a preventive of good schools. Still the results have been
marvellous. Out of 448 cities in the United States, with a
population each of 8,000 and over, only 73 are in the South.

Of 28, with a population from 100,000 to 1,500,000, only 2 (St. Louis being excluded) are in the South. Of 96, with a population between 25,000 and 100,000, 17 are in the South. The urban population is comparatively small, and agriculture is the chief occupation. Of 858,000 negroes in Georgia, 130,000 are in cities and towns, and 728,000 in the country; in Mississippi, urban colored population, 42,000, rural, 700,000; in South Carolina, urban, 74,000, rural, 615,000; in North Carolina, urban, 66,000, against 198,000 rural; in Alabama, 65,000 against 613,000; in Louisiana, 93,000 against 466,000. The schools for colored children are maintained on an average 89.2 days in a year, and for white children 98.6, but the preponderance of the white over the black race, in towns and cities, helps in part to explain the difference. While the colored population supplies less than its due proportion of pupils to the public schools, and the regularity of attendance is less than with the white, yet the difference in length of school term in schools for white and schools for black children is trifling. In the same grades the wages of teachers are about the same. The annual State school revenue is apportioned impartially among white and black children, so much per capita to each child. In the rural districts the colored people are dependent chiefly upon the State apportionment, which is by law devoted mainly to the payment of teachers' salaries. Hence, the school-houses and other conveniences in the country for the negroes are inferior, but in the cities the appropriation for schools is general and is allotted to white and colored, according to the needs of each. A small proportion of the school fund comes from colored sources. All the States do not discriminate in assessments of taxable property, but in Georgia, where the ownership is ascertained, the negroes returned in 1892 $11,869,575 of taxable property against $448,883,959 returned by white owners. The amount of property listed for taxation in North Carolina in 1894 was, by white citizens, $234,109,568; by colored citizens, $8,018,446. To an inquiry for official data, the auditor of the State of Virginia

says: "The taxes collected in 1891 from white citizens were
$2,991,646.24, and from the colored, $163,175.67. The
amount paid for public schools for whites, $588,564.87; for
negroes, $309,364.15. Add $15,000 for Colored Normal and
$80,000 for colored lunatic asylum. Apportioning the crimi-
nal expenses between the white and the colored people in the
ratio of convicts of each race received into the Penitentiary
in 1891, and it shows that the criminal expenses put upon
the State annually by the whites are $55,749.57 and by the
negroes $204,018.99."

Of the desire of the colored people for education the proof
is conclusive, and of their capacity to receive mental culture
there is not the shade of a reason to support an adverse
hypothesis. The Bureau of Education furnishes the following
suggestive table:

SIXTEEN FORMER SLAVE STATES AND THE DISTRICT OF COLUMBIA.

Year.	Common-School Enrollment.		Expenditures.
	White.	Colored.	Both Races
1876–77	1,827,139	571,506	$11,231,073
1877–78	2,051,946	675,150	12,695,091
1878–79	2,013,684	685,942	12,474,141
1879–80	2,215,674	784,709	12,675,685
1880–81	2,234,877	802,374	13,656,844
1881–82	2,249,263	802,982	15,241,740
1882–83	2,370,110	817,240	16,363,471
1883–84	2,546,448	1,002,313	17,884,558
1884–85	2,676,911	1,030,463	19,263,874
1885–86	2,773,145	1,048,659	20,208,143
1886–87	2,975,773	1,118,556	20,824,969
1887–88	3,110,606	1,140,405	21,810,178
1888–89	3,197,830	1,213,092	23,171,878
1889–90	3,402,420	1,296,959	24,880,107
1890–91	3,570,624	1,329,549	26,600,310
1891–92	3,607,549	1,354,316	27,691,488

Total amount expended in 16 years, $295,851,470.

In 1890–91 there were 79,962 white teachers and 24,150
colored. To the enrollment in common schools should be
added 30,000 colored children, who are in normal or secondary

schools. The amount expended for education of negroes is not stated separately, but Dr. W. T. Harris estimates that there must have been nearly $75,000,000 expended by the Southern States, in addition to what has been contributed by missionary and philanthropic sources. In Virginia, North Carolina, Georgia, Florida, Alabama, Mississippi, Louisiana, Texas, and Arkansas, annual grants are made for the support of colored normal and industrial schools.

The negroes must rely very largely upon the public schools for their education, and so they should. They are, and will continue to be, the most efficient factors for uplifting the race. The States, at immense sacrifice, with impartial liberality, have taxed themselves for a population which contributes very little to the State revenues, and nothing could be done more prejudicial to the educational interests of the colored people than to indulge in any hostility or indifference to, or neglect of, these free schools. Denominations and individuals can do nothing more harmful to the race than to foster opposition to the public schools.

XII. A potential agency in enlightening public opinion and in working out the problem of the education of the negro has been the John F. Slater Fund. " In view of the apprehensions felt by all thoughtful persons," when the duties and privileges of citizenship were suddenly thrust upon millions of lately emancipated slaves, Mr. Slater conceived the purpose of giving a large sum of money to their proper education. After deliberate reflection and much conference, he selected a Board of Trust and placed in their hands a million of dollars. This unique gift, originating wholly with himself, and elaborated in his own mind in most of its details, was for " the uplifting of the lately emancipated population of the Southern States and their posterity, by conferring on them the blessings of Christian education." " Not only for their own sake, but also for the sake of our common country," he sought to provide " the means of such education as shall tend to make them good men and good citizens," associating the instruction of the mind " with training in just notions of duty toward God and

man, in the light of the Holy Scriptures." Leaving to the
corporation the largest discretion and liberty, in the prosecu-
tion of the general object, as described in his Letter of Trust,
he yet indicated as "lines of operation adapted to the condition of things" the encouragement of "institutions as are
most effectually useful in promoting the training of teachers."
The Trust was to be administered "in no partisan, sectional,
or sectarian spirit, but in the interest of a generous patriotism
and an enlightened Christian spirit." Soon after organization
the Trustees expressed very strongly their judgment that the
scholars should be "trained in some manual occupation,
simultaneously with their mental and moral instruction," and
aid was confined to such institutions as gave "instruction in
trades and other manual occupations," that the pupils might
obtain an intelligent mastery of the indispensable elements of
industrial success. So repeated have been similar declarations
on the part of the Trustees and the General Agents that manual training, or education in industries, may be regarded as
an unalterable policy; but only such institutions were to be
aided as were, "with good reason, believed to be on a permanent basis." Mr. Slater explained "Christian Education,"
as used in his Letter of Gift, to be teaching, "leavened with
a predominant and salutary Christian influence," such as was
found in "the common school teaching of Massachusetts and
Connecticut," and that there was "no need of limiting the
gifts of the Fund to denominational institutions." Since the
first appropriation, near fifty different institutions have been
aided, in sums ranging from $500 to $5,000. As required by
the Founder, neither principal nor income is expended for
land or buildings. For a few years aid was given in buying
machinery or apparatus, but now the income is applied almost
exclusively to paying the salaries of teachers engaged in the normal or industrial work. The number of aided institutions has
been lessened, with the view of concentrating and making more
effective the aid and of improving the instruction in normal and
industrial work. The table appended presents a summary of the
appropriations which have been made from year to year.

CASH DISBURSED BY JOHN F. SLATER FUND, AS
APPROPRIATIONS FOR EDUCATIONAL
INSTITUTIONS.

To August	13, 1884	$	24,881.66
" April	30, 1885		30,414.19
" "	1886		38,724.98
" "	1887		39,816.28
" "	1888		46,183.34
" "	1889		43,709.98
" "	1890		41,560.02
" "	1891		50,650.00
" "	1892		45,816.33
" "	1893		37,475.00
" "	1894		40,750.00
			$439,981.78

JOHN MURPHY & CO., PRINTERS,
BALTIMORE.

STATISTICS OF THE NEGROES

IN THE

UNITED STATES

BY

HENRY GANNETT

OF THE UNITED STATES GEOLOGICAL SURVEY

BALTIMORE

PUBLISHED BY THE TRUSTEES

1894

ANNOUNCEMENT.

The Trustees of the John F. Slater Fund propose to publish from time to time papers that relate to the education of the colored race. These papers are designed to furnish information to those who are concerned in the administration of schools, and also to those who by their official stations are called upon to act or to advise in respect to the care of such institutions.

The Trustees believe that the experimental period in the education of the blacks is drawing to a close. Certain principles that were doubted thirty years ago now appear to be generally recognized as sound. In the next thirty years better systems will undoubtedly prevail, and the aid of the separate States is likely to be more and more freely bestowed. There will also be abundant room for continued generosity on the part of individuals and associations. It is to encourage and assist the workers and the thinkers that these papers will be published.

Each paper, excepting the first number (made up chiefly of official documents), will be the utterance of the writer whose name is attached to it, the Trustees disclaiming in advance all responsibility for the statement of facts and opinions.

THE TRUSTEES OF THE JOHN F. SLATER FUND

OCCASIONAL PAPERS, No. 4

STATISTICS OF THE NEGROES

IN THE

UNITED STATES

BY

HENRY GANNETT

OF THE UNITED STATES GEOLOGICAL SURVEY

BALTIMORE

PUBLISHED BY THE TRUSTEES

1894

The statistics in the following paper have been examined by Hon. Carroll D. Wright, Superintendent of the Census of the United States, and are published with his approbation. He was not requested to express an opinion in respect to the author's views,—nor has he done so.

ANNOUNCEMENT

The Trustees of the John F. Slater Fund propose to publish from time to time papers that relate to the education of the colored race. These papers are designed to furnish information to those who are concerned in the administration of schools, and also to those who by their official stations are called upon to act or to advise in respect to the care of such institutions.

The Trustees believe that the experimental period in the education of the blacks is drawing to a close. Certain principles that were doubted thirty years ago now appear to be generally recognized as sound. In the next thirty years better systems will undoubtedly prevail, and the aid of the separate States is likely to be more and more freely bestowed. There will also be abundant room for continued generosity on the part of individuals and associations. It is to encourage and assist the workers and the thinkers that these papers will be published.

Each paper, excepting the first number (made up chiefly of official documents), will be the utterance of the writer whose name is attached to it, the Trustees disclaiming in advance all responsibility for the statement of facts and opinions.

A STATISTICAL SKETCH OF THE NEGROES IN THE UNITED STATES.

INTRODUCTION.

From the time of the earliest settlements upon these shores, the United States has contained two elements of population, the white race and the negro race. These two races have together peopled this country, increasing partly by accessions to their numbers from abroad and partly by natural increase, until to-day (1894) the white race numbers probably 61,000,000 and the negroes 8,000,000. The history of the latter race, thus brought into close association with a more civilized and stronger people for two and three-fourths centuries, is one of surpassing interest. Unfortunately, however, this history, for the earlier part of the period, is, with the exception of a few fragments, utterly lost. For the last century, however, since the year 1790, the date of the first United States census, we have, at ten-year intervals, pictures of the distribution of the race, and considerable information regarding its social condition.

SLAVE TRADE.

The slave trade flourished actively up to the close of the last century, and indeed it did not entirely cease until the year 1808. It was mainly in the hands of the English, including their North American colonies. It was a large and flourishing business for the ship-owners of New England, and the wealth of many of the families of those colonies originated in this traffic.

Of the number of slaves brought from Africa to this country, either directly or by way of the West India Islands, we have very little information. Prior to 1788 there are no records, and since that time the records of the slave trade do not distinguish between the slaves brought to the United States and those to other parts of America.

Of the number of slaves in this country in colonial times the information is almost equally scanty, consisting of little more than estimates by different historical writers. Of these, Bancroft's are perhaps as reliable as any. His estimates of the number of negroes at different times are as follows:

```
1750 . . .         . . . . . . . . . . . . . . . 220,000
1754 . . .         . . . . . . . . . . . . . . . 260,000
1760 . .           . . . . . . . . . . . . . . . 310,000
1770 . . . . .     . . . . . . . . . . . . . . . 462,000
1780 . . . . . . . . . . . . . . . . . . . . . . 562,000
```

NUMBERS OF EACH RACE.

In 1790 we have the first reliable data regarding the number and distribution of the negroes. The total number of each race at this and each succeeding decennial enumeration is shown in the following table:

CENSUS YEAR.	WHITE.	NEGRO.
1790	3,172,006	757,208
1800	4,306,446	1,002,037
1810	5,862,073	1,377,808
1820	7,862,166	1,771,656
1830	10,537,378	2,328,642
1840	14,195,805	2,873,648
1850	19,553,068	3,638,808
1860	26,922,537	4,441,830
1870	33,589,377	4,880,009
1880	43,402,970	6,580,793
1890	54,983,890	7,470,040

From this it appears that the whites have increased in a century from a little over 3,000,000 to nearly 55,000,000, and the negroes from three-fourths of a million to about seven and one-half millions. The whites were in 1890 nearly eighteen times as numerous as in 1790, the negroes nearly ten times as numerous.

The diagram constituting Plate I presents the same facts in graphic form. In each case the total length of the bar is proportional to the total population in the year indicated. The white portion of each bar represents the white population of the country, while the shaded portion represents the negro population.

The tables and diagram illustrate the rapid growth of the country in population, both of its white and its negro element.

PROPORTIONS OF EACH RACE.

The following table shows the proportions in which the total population was made up of these two elements at each census, expressed in percentages of the total population:

CENSUS YEAR.	WHITE.	NEGRO.
1790	80.73	19.27
1800	81.12	18.88
1810	80.97	19.03
1820	81.61	18.39
1830	81.90	18.10
1840	83.16	16.84
1850	84.31	15.69
1860	85.62	14.13
1870	87.11	12.66
1880	86.54	13.12
1890	87.80	11.93

This table and Plate II show that on the whole the negroes have diminished decidedly in proportion to the whites. In 1790 they formed 19.27 per cent. or very nearly one-fifth of the whole population. At the end of this century they constituted only 11.93 per cent., or less than one-eighth of the population. At the end of the century their proportion was less than two-thirds as large as at this beginning. Moreover, this diminution in the proportion has been almost unbroken from the beginning to the end of the century. The proportion of the negroes has apparently increased in only two out of the eleven censuses, namely in 1810, immediately after the cessation of the slave trade, and in 1880. I say apparently, because in the latter case the increase is only apparent, due to a deficient enumeration of this race in the census preceding, namely, that of 1870.

RATES OF INCREASE.

The following table and the diagram accompanying it show the rates of increase of the negroes during each of the ten-year periods for the last century, and placed in juxtaposition therewith for comparison are the rates of increase of the whites of the entire country.

DECADE.	PERCENTAGE OF INCREASE.	
	WHITE.	NEGRO.
1790 to 1800	35.76	32.33
1800 to 1810	36.12	37.50
1810 to 1820	34.12	28.59
1820 to 1830	34.03	31.44
1830 to 1840	34.72	23.40
1840 to 1850	37.74	26.63
1850 to 1860	37.69	22.07
1860 to 1870	24.76	9.86
1870 to 1880	29.22	34.85
1880 to 1890	26.68	13.51

Rates of Increase of White and Negro Population.

Per Cent.

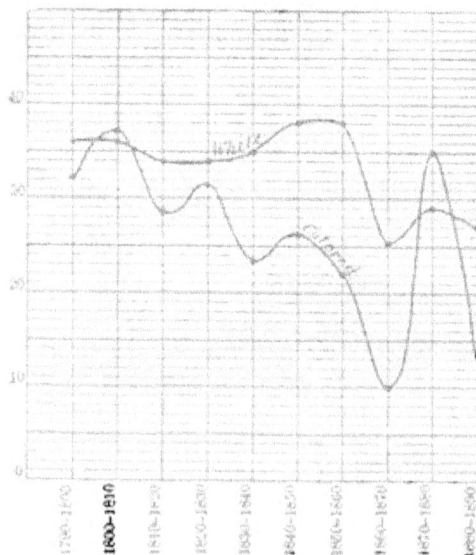

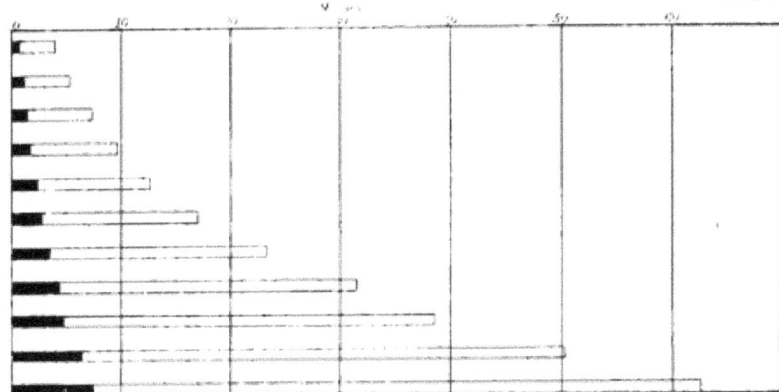

TOTAL POPULATION AND WHITE AND NEGRO ELEMENTS

PLATE I.

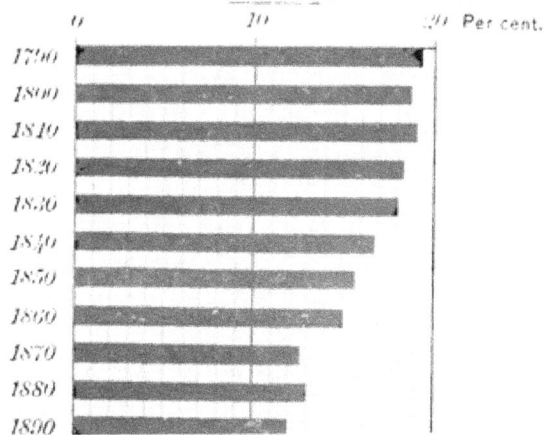

PLATE II.

PROPORTION OF THE NEGRO ELEMENT TO THE TOTAL POPULATION.

0   10   20 Per cent.

1790
1800
1810
1820
1830
1840
1850
1860
1870
1880
1890

This table and diagram show that, with the exception of two ten-year periods, namely, those from 1800 to 1810 and 1870 to 1880, the negro element has in every case increased at a less rapid rate than the white element, and in many cases its rate of increase has been very much smaller.

Thus a comparison of the numerical progress of the negroes with that of the whites in the country, as a whole, shows that the former have not held their own, but have constantly fallen behind. They have not increased as rapidly as the whites.

It may be said that this is due to the enormous immigration which certain parts of the country has received, an immigration composed entirely of whites. This suggestion can easily be tested. White immigration on a considerable scale began about 1847. Prior to that time it was not of importance. We may then divide the century into two equal parts and contrast the relative rates of increase of the races during those half-centuries. Between 1790 and 1840 the whites increased 4.5 times, the negroes 3.8 times. The latter element had diminished in relative importance in this half-century from about one-fifth of the population to one-sixth.

In the succeeding fifty years the whites had increased 3.9 times and the colored 2.6 times only. In other words, the greater increase of the whites has not been dependent upon immigration, since their rate of increase was greater than that of the negroes before immigration set in.

These figures, and the conclusions necessarily derived from them, should set at rest forever all fears regarding any possible conflict between the two races. We have before us the testimony of a century to show us that the negroes, while in no danger of extinction, while increasing at a rate probably more rapid than in any other part of the earth, are yet increasing less rapidly than the white people of the country, and to demonstrate that the latter will become more and more numerically the dominant race in America. Whether the negro will, through an improvement in his social condition, become of greater importance relatively to his numbers is a matter to be discussed later

CENTER OF POPULATION.

The center of population, as it is called, may be described as the center of gravity of the inhabitants as they are distributed at the time under consideration, each inhabitant being supposed to have the same weight and to press downwards with a force proportional to his distance from this center.

The center of population of all the inhabitants of the United States has been computed for each census. At the time of the first census, in 1790, the center of population was found to be in Maryland, on the eastern shore of Chesapeake Bay, nearly opposite Baltimore. The general westward movement of population has caused a corresponding westward movement of this center, such movement following very nearly the line of the 39th parallel of north latitude. In 1880 the center of the total population was found on the south bank of the Ohio river, nearly opposite Cincinnati, and in 1890 it was found in southern Indiana, twenty miles east of Columbus, in latitude 39 12′ and in longitude 85°33′.

The center of the negro population has been computed in 1880 and in 1890. At the first of these dates it was found in latitude 34 42′ and in longitude 84°58′. This position is in the northwestern corner of Georgia, not far from Dalton. In 1890 it was found to have moved southwestward into latitude 34 26′ and longitude 85°18′, being not far from the boundary between Alabama and Georgia and a few miles west of Rome, Ga. The longitude of the center of the negro population was very nearly the same as that of the total population, but in latitude it was nearly five degrees, or more than 300 miles south of it. The positions of the center of total population and of the negro population in 1880 and in 1890 are shown upon the map which constitutes Plate VI.

The movements of the center of population are the net resultant of all the movements of population. During the past decade the negroes have moved in all directions, north, south, east, and west, but, as indicated by the movement of the center, the net resultant of their movements has been toward the southwest. As a whole this element moved in a southwesterly direction a distance of about 25 miles.

FREE NEGROES AND SLAVES.

Prior to 1870 the negro element, as returned by the successive censuses, was made up of two parts, free negroes and slaves. The proportions of these elements differed at different times, as is shown by the first column in the following table.

	Per cent. which free negroes bore to all negroes.	Per cent. of all free negroes found in former slave states.	Per cent. of all free negroes found in free states.
1790	8.	55	45
1800	11.	56	44
1810	13.5	58	42
1820	13.	57	43
1830	14.	57	43
1840	13.	56	44
1850	12.	55	45
1860	11.	54	46

From this it appears that the free negroes constituted in 1790 only 8 per cent. of all negroes, that the proportion increased rapidly to 1830, when they constituted not less than 14 per cent., and from that time the proportion diminished until in 1860 they constituted 11 per cent. of all negroes.

Moreover, the proportions of the free negroes found within the slave states and the free states differed at different times, as is shown by the second and third columns of the above table. The second column shows that on the whole considerably more than half of the free negroes were found within the former slave states and less than one-half within the free states, and that the proportion of free negroes which were found in the former slave states ranged from 54 per cent. in 1860 to 58 per cent. in 1810.

DISTRIBUTION OF THE NEGRO ELEMENT.

The negroes are distributed very unequally over the country. While they are found in every state and territory and

in almost every county of the land, the vast body of them
are found in the southern states, in those states lying south
of Mason and Dixon's line, the Ohio river, the northern
boundary of Missouri, and westward as far as Texas and
Arkansas. The two maps upon Plate III illustrate their
distribution, state by state, over the country. One of these
maps shows their density, that is, the average number in
each square mile. It is an absolute measure of their numbers in different parts of the country. It is seen that they
are the most plentiful in Maryland, Virginia, South Carolina,
and Mississippi, and secondarily in North Carolina, Tennessee, Georgia, Alabama, and Louisiana. On the other hand,
in nearly all the northern and western states they are very
sparsely distributed, there being in these states, with scarcely
an exception, less than four of them to a square mile, while
in many of them there is less than one to a square mile.

The other map shows the proportion which the negro
element bears to the total population, state by state. This
is a measure of its importance relative to the whites.
From this map it is seen that in three states, Louisiana,
Mississippi, and South Carolina, more than half the people
are negroes. Indeed, in South Carolina three out of every
five of the inhabitants are of this race. It is seen further
that in all the states along the Atlantic and Gulf, from Virginia to Louisiana, together with Arkansas, more than one-
fourth of the people are negroes, while, on the other hand,
throughout the entire north and west the proportion of
negroes is less than five per cent., and in many of the states
it is less than one per cent. of the total population.

Proportion of the Negroes in the Slave States.

The distribution of the negro race may be still more closely
characterized by the statement that in 1890 there were found
in the former slave states not less than 92 per cent. of
all negroes. This proportion has differed at different times
during the last century, as is shown in the following table.

PLATE III

PROPORTION OF NEGROES TO TOTAL POPULATION IN 1890

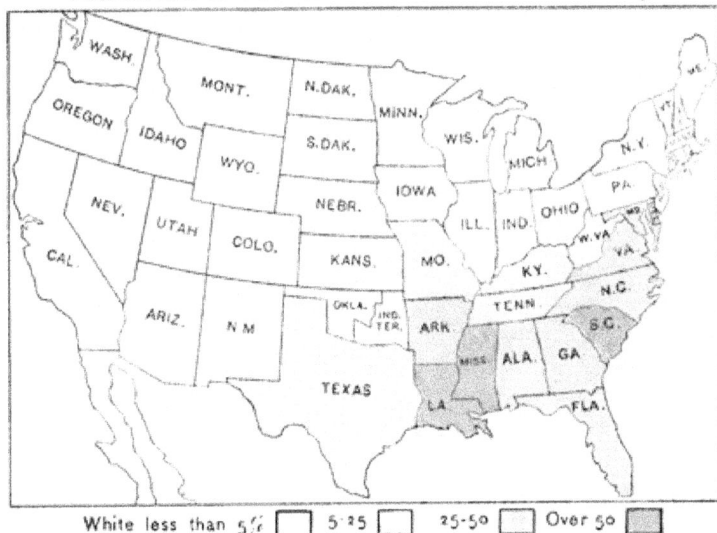

White less than 5% ☐ 5-25 ☐ 25-50 ☐ Over 50 ▨

DENSITY OF NEGRO POPULATION IN 1890.

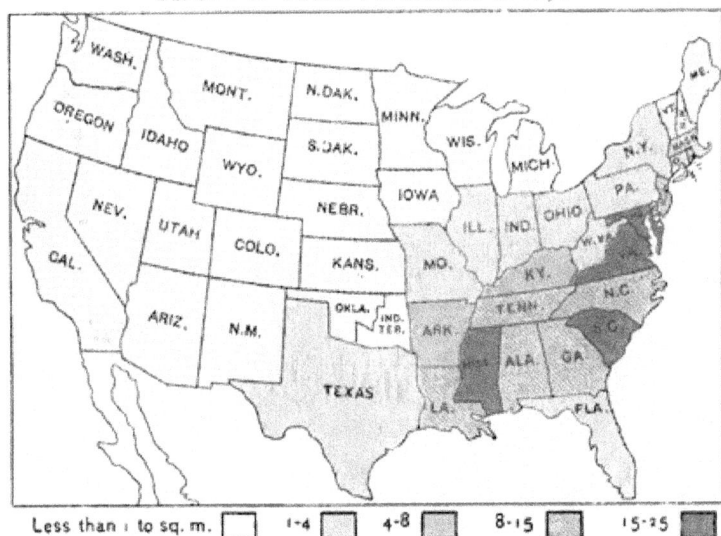

Less than 1 to sq. m. ☐ 1-4 ☐ 4-8 ☐ 8-15 ☐ 15-25 ▨

PROPORTION OF TOTAL NEGRO ELEMENT COMPRISED IN FORMER SLAVE STATES.

YEAR.	PER CENT.
1790	91
1800	91
1810	92
1820	93
1830	93
1840	94
1850	95
1860	95
1870	94
1880	93
1890	92

From this table it will be seen that at the commencement of this history the former slave states contained 91 per cent. of the negroes of the country. As time wore on this proportion increased until in 1850 and 1860 they comprised 95 per cent., or nineteen-twentieths of all, while since that date, *i. e.* during the period of freedom of the race, it has shown a slight tendency northward, the proportion in the former slave states having become reduced, as above stated, to 92 per cent.

THE NEGROES OF THE SLAVE STATES.

In the above pages the history of the negroes has been traced in a broad general way and compared with that of the entire population and the white element of the country. The history is more or less complicated with the results of immigration, and with other disturbing factors, which have affected mainly the north and west. We may now without serious error confine our study of the race to the southern states, the former slaveholding states, in which are found more than nine-tenths of the whole number of the negroes. The movement of these people from the south into the north has been inconsiderable, and there has been but little movement of the whites in either direction across the boundary line between the sections. The south has received little immigration either from the north or from Europe, and the emigration from it has been unimportant. So far as emigration and immigration are concerned it has been throughout our history almost isolated from the rest of the world. So we may without serious error study the relations of the whites and blacks of this region by itself, without reference to other parts of the country.

PROPORTIONS OF THE RACES.

The following table and accompanying diagram (Plate IV) show the proportions in which the population of this part of the United States was composed at each census for the past hundred years

PROPORTIONS IN WHICH THE POPULATION OF FORMER SLAVE STATES WAS MADE UP.

	WHITE.	NEGRO.
1790	65	35
1800	65	35
1810	63	37
1820	63	37
1830	63	37
1840	63	37
1850	64	36
1860	66	34
1870	68	32
1880	67	33
1890	69	31

It appears from the above table that a century ago the population of the South was made up of whites and negroes in the proportions of 65 and 35 per cent., and that in 1890 the proportions were 69 and 31 per cent. The proportion of negroes increased from 1790 to 1810, when it reached 37 per cent., leaving only 63 per cent. as the proportion of the whites, and remained practically stationary for three decades. Since 1840 the proportion of negroes has diminished.

RATES OF INCREASE.

The following table, showing the rates of increase of the two races for each ten-year period during the past century, leads to a similar conclusion, that is, that for a half-century the negroes increased more rapidly than the whites, while during the last half-century they have increased less rapidly.

PROPORTION OF NEGROES TO TOTAL POPULATION IN 1890

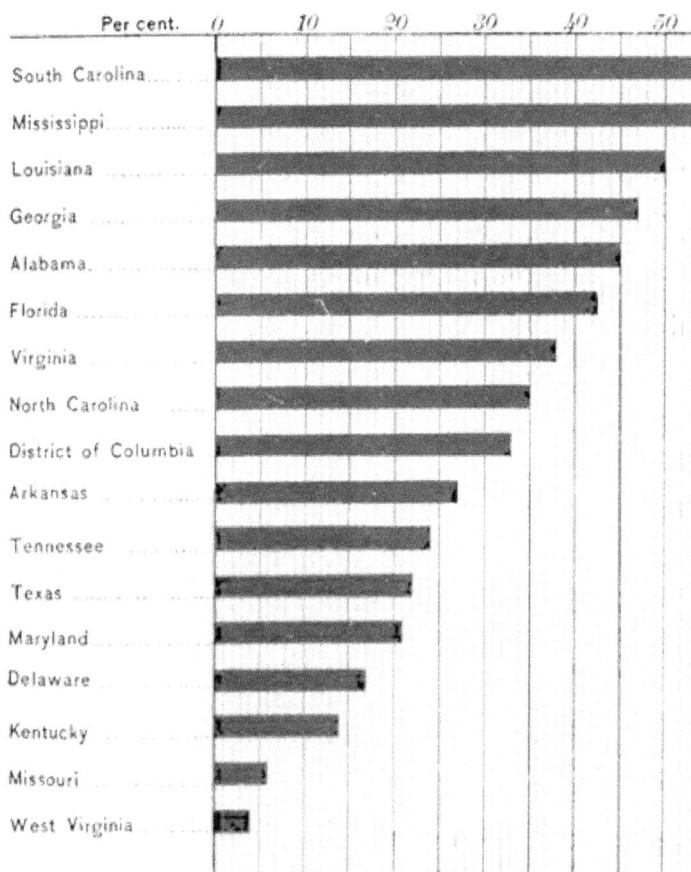

Per cent.	0	10	20	30	40	50

South Carolina

Mississippi

Louisiana

Georgia

Alabama

Florida

Virginia

North Carolina

District of Columbia

Arkansas

Tennessee

Texas

Maryland

Delaware

Kentucky

Missouri

West Virginia

Proportion which negroes of former slave states bore to
population of those states.

Per cent.

0	10	20	30

RATES OF INCREASE OF WHITE AND NEGRO ELEMENTS OF FORMER SLAVE STATES.

		WHITE.	NEGRO.
1790 to 1800	 34		33
1800 to 1810	 30		39
1810 to 1820	 28		30
1820 to 1830	 29		32
1830 to 1840	 27		24
1840 to 1850	 34		27
1850 to 1860	 30		22
1860 to 1870	 17		8
1870 to 1880	 33		34
1880 to 1890	 24		13

THE NEGROES IN CITIES.

It is well known that as the population of a state or country increases, such increase goes in constantly rising proportion into its cities; in other words, that urban population increases at a more rapid rate than the total population, especially after the population has passed a certain average density. This country presents an excellent example of this tendency of population towards the cities. At the time of the first census only 3½ per cent. of the total population was in cities of 8000 inhabitants or more, while in 1890, a century later, the proportion in cities had increased to over 29 per cent. The total population of the country had become very nearly 16 times as great, while its urban element had become 139 times as great. The latter had increased more than 8 times as rapidly as the former.

Having thus illustrated the general tendency of the people towards cities, it will be instructive to see how the negroes have behaved in this regard. In measuring their appetency for urban life I shall consider only the population of the former slave states, and shall contrast the negro with the white element of those states in this regard. I shall follow the practice of the Census Office also in considering as urban the inhabitants of cities of 8000 or more.

In cities of 8000 inhabitants or more there were found in 1860 only 4.2 per cent. of the negroes of these states, while of the whites 10.9 per cent. were found at that time in these cities. The violent social changes attendant upon the war produced, among other results, an extensive migration of negroes to the cities, so that in 1870 the proportion of them found in cities had more than doubled, being no less than 8.5 per cent., while of the whites there were found 13.1 per cent. In 1880 the proportion of negroes in cities had diminished to 8.4 per cent., while that of the whites had also diminished, being 12.4 per cent.

The census of 1890 shows a decided increase in the proportion of each race in the cities, that of the negroes being 12 per cent. and that of the whites being 15.7 per cent.

Thus it is seen that the proportion of the negroes in the cities has in every case been less than that of the whites, but that they have gained upon the whites in this regard. This gain is, however, very slight and is probably not significant. While the negro is extremely gregarious and is by that instinct drawn toward the great centers of population, on the other hand he is not fitted either by nature or education for those vocations for the pursuit of which men collect in cities, that is, for manufactures and commerce. The inclinations of this race, drawn from its inheritance, tend to keep it wedded to the soil, and the probabilities are that as cities increase in these states in number and size, and with them manufactures and commerce develop, the great body of the negroes will continue to remain aloof from them and cultivate the soil as heretofore.

GEOGRAPHICAL DISTRIBUTION.

The geographical environment of the negro has been made a subject of careful study by the Census Office, and many interesting facts regarding its distribution with reference to topography, altitude, rainfall, and temperature have been developed.

It is found that more than 17 per cent. of them live in the low, swampy regions of the Atlantic coast and in the alluvial region in the Mississippi valley. This proportion contrasts sharply with that of the total population, of which only 4 per cent. are found in these regions. Upon the Atlantic plain the proportion of negroes is also much greater than that of the total population, and, generally speaking, it may be said that they seek low, moist regions and avoid mountainous country. This peculiarity of their distribution is brought out more forcibly in their distribution with reference to elevation above sea-level. At an altitude less than 100 feet above the sea there are found nearly one-fourth of the negroes, while only about one-sixth of the total population is in these regions. Below 500 feet are found seven-tenths, while nearly two-fifths of the total population are found at this altitude. Again, below 1000 feet there are found 94.5 per cent. of all the negroes of the country, while of the total population there are found only 77 per cent. below that altitude.

It is, of course, well known that the negroes prefer higher temperatures than the white race. A measure of this is given by the statement that while the total population lives, on an average, under a mean annual temperature of 53 degrees Fah., that under which the negro lives is, on an average, 61 degrees, or not less than 8 degrees higher. The great body of the negroes live where the mean annual temperature ranges from 55 degrees to 70 degrees, very nearly 85 per cent. of this element being found within the region thus defined.

Nothing perhaps more sharply characterizes the difference in the habitat of the negroes and the element of foreign birth than the difference in temperature conditions under which they are found; a difference which may be characterized by the following statement: In those regions where the annual temperature exceeds 55 degrees are found seven-eighths of the negroes. On the other hand, in those regions where the temperature is less than 55 degrees are found nine-tenths of the foreign-born.

Those who are acquainted with the relations between the distribution of population and rainfall over the surface of the country are aware that the great body of the negroes is found in regions of heavy rainfall. Indeed, more than nine-tenths of their numbers are found where it exceeds 40 inches annually, and more than three-fifths where it exceeds 50 inches. These figures are greatly in excess of those concerning the total population.

History of the Negro in each Slave State.

Thus far the distribution and history of the race have been considered broadly. It will now be of interest to take up each of the former slave states individually and trace the history of the race within its limits. This is summarized in the following table and group of diagrams (Plate V), which present in each of the former slave states the proportion which the negro element bore to the total population at each census.

For economy of space the black bars representing the proportions in the diagrams are not extended to their full length, so the lengths of the bars do not represent the absolute percentage which the negroes bear to the total population. Since we are interested mainly in the relative lengths of the different bars of each state, and not in comparing those of one state with those of another, this is a matter of no consequence.

In Delaware the proportion of negroes in 1790 was about 22 per cent. This proportion increased gradually until 1840, when it was 25 per cent. Since then it has diminished and in 1890 was about 17 per cent. In Maryland over one-third of the population were negroes in 1790. The proportion increased and reached a maximum in 1810, when it was 38 per cent. Since then it has diminished, and in 1890 was but 21 per cent. In the District of Columbia the proportion of negroes in 1800, the first year of record, was about 29 per cent. It reached its maximum with 33 per cent. in 1810, and from that time steadily diminished until the opening of the Civil War. In 1860 the proportion was 19 per cent. During the war large numbers of negroes took refuge within the Capital, increasing the proportion to about one-third of the total population, which ratio has been maintained.

In Kentucky one-sixth of the population were negroes in 1790. The proportion increased until 1830, when it was about one-fourth of the population, since which time it has diminished and is at present but 14 per cent.

In Tennessee only one-tenth of the population were negroes at the time of the first census. That proportion steadily increased for 90 years, reaching its maximum in 1880, when it slightly exceeded one-fourth of the population. In the last ten years it has diminished a trifle.

The first report of population regarding Missouri was made in 1810. At that time about one-sixth of the inhabitants were negroes. In 1830 the proportion was slightly greater. Since then it has diminished rapidly and in 1890 the negroes constituted less than 6 per cent. of the population.

In the state of Virginia the negroes constituted in 1790 not less than 41 per cent. of the inhabitants, and their proportion increased slightly for 20 years, reaching a maximum in 1810 of over 43 per cent. Since that time it has diminished steadily and in 1890 constituted but 27½ per cent., taking the states of Virginia and West Virginia together.

All the above are border states, and all, with the exception of Tennessee and the District of Columbia, show a similar history. They show an increase in the proportion for two, three, or four of the earlier decades, and then a constant and great diminution in the proportion. The other states show a very different history. North Carolina, starting with 27 per cent., has increased slowly and with some slight oscillations up to 1880, when the proportion reached 38 per cent. In the last decade it has diminished. South Carolina, starting with 44 per cent., increased her proportion until 1880, when more than three-fifths of the population were negroes. Since then there has been a trifling diminution. Georgia started with 36 per cent., and with some slight oscillations continued to increase until 1880. Within the last ten years there has been a slight reduction. In Florida the oscillations have been considerable. The history commenced with

1830, when 47 per cent. of the population were negroes. It reached a maximum of 49 per cent. at the next census, followed by a diminution for two decades. Then in 1870 it rose again to 49 per cent., since which time it has diminished rapidly, especially during the decade between 1880 and 1890. The history of Alabama commenced in 1820, when one-third of her people were negroes. The proportion increased up to 1870, and since then has diminished. Mississippi's history began in 1800, when 41 per cent. of her people were negroes, and with some slight oscillations the proportion has increased up to the present time. The history of Louisiana commenced in 1810, when 55 per cent. of her population were negroes. Her history has been a diversified one, the maximum proportion of this race being reached in 1830 with 59 per cent. Since that time it has, on the whole, diminished, and in 1890 half the people of the State were negroes. The history of Texas began in 1850, when 28 per cent. of her people were negroes. The proportion increased for two decades, when it reached 31 per cent. Since that time it has diminished rapidly, owing largely to immigration to the central parts of the state. The history of Arkansas begins in 1820, when a little less than one-eighth of its people were negroes. The proportion has increased almost continuously from that time to the present, and in 1890 the negroes formed 27 per cent. of the total population.

Thus it is seen that in the cotton states the proportion of the negro element has in nearly all cases increased until a very recent time. Indeed, in two or three of them it has increased up to the time of the last census, while in most of them the only diminution in the proportion has occurred during the last ten years. All this indicates in the most unmistakable terms a general southward migration of this race. As compared with the whites, the border states have lost in proportion of negroes for the past half-century, while the cotton states have continued to gain until very recently.

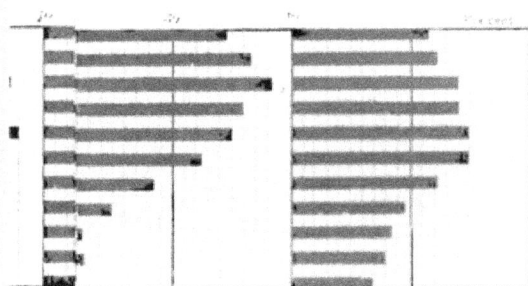

Maryland

Tennessee   North Carolina

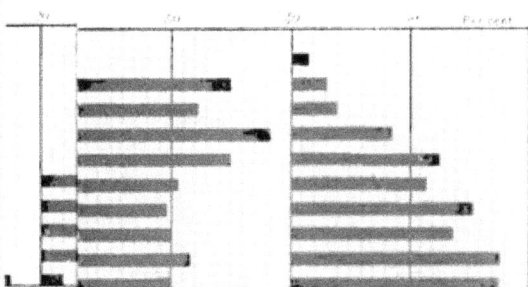

Louisiana   Mississippi

The
Internet Archive
Birney Collection
Digitization Project

Notice to
OCA Camera
Operator

☐ Foldout

page_____

☐ Missing Page

page_____

☐ Photocopy

page_____

☐ Brittle/Discolored
Paper

page_____

☐ Other problem:

Specify: _____

page_____

Specify: _____

page_____

Specify: _____

page_____

PERCENTAGE OF NEGROES TO TOTAL POPULATION.

STATES.	1890.	1880.	1870.	1860.	1850.	1840.	1830.	1820.	1810.	1800.	1790.
Delaware	16.85	18.04	18.23	19.27	22.25	25.00	24.35	24.01	23.82	22.44	21.64
Maryland	20.69	22.49	22.46	24.91	28.32	32.30	34.88	36.12	38.22	36.66	34.74
District of Col'bia	32.80	33.55	32.96	19.67	26.59	24.85	30.81	31.55	33.67	28.57	·
Kentucky	14.42	16.46	16.82	20.44	22.49	24.31	24.73	22.95	20.24	18.59	17.03
Tennessee	24.37	26.14	25.61	25.50	24.52	22.74	21.43	19.60	17.52	13.16	10.59
Missouri	5.61	6.70	6.86	10.03	13.20	15.58	18.33	15.78	17.25	·	·
Virginia } West Virginia }	27.51	30.85	31.84	34.39	37.06	40.23	42.69	43.38	43.41	41.57	40.86
North Carolina	34.67	37.96	36.56	36.42	36.26	35.64	35.93	34.28	32.24	29.35	36.81
South Carolina	59.85	60.70	58.93	58.59	58.93	56.43	55.63	52.77	48.40	43.21	43.72
Georgia	46.74	47.02	46.04	44.05	42.41	41.63	42.57	44.41	42.40	37.14	35.93
Florida	42.46	47.01	48.81	44.63	46.02	48.71	47.06	·	·	·	·
Alabama	44.84	47.53	47.69	45.40	44.73	43.26	38.48	32.19	·	·	·
Mississippi	57.58	57.47	53.65	55.28	51.24	52.33	48.44	44.30	42.94	41.48	·
Louisiana	49.99	51.46	50.10	49.49	50.65	55.04	58.54	52.01	55.18	·	·
Texas	21.84	24.71	29.97	30.27	27.54	·	·	·	·	·	·
Arkansas	27.40	26.25	25.22	25.55	22.73	20.01	15.52	11.73	·	·	·

DETAILS OF MOVEMENTS OF NEGROES BETWEEN 1880 AND 1890.

The map upon Plate VI shows the movements of this race in detail during the ten years between 1880 and 1890, within the former slave states. The northern part of Missouri and western Texas are not represented upon this map, inasmuch as the number of negroes in these regions is not large.

The areas upon this map which have the darkest shade are those in which the number of negroes has absolutely diminished during the decade in question. The areas in the lightest tint are those in which the negroes have increased, but at a rate less than the increase of the same element in the country at large. The areas of medium tint are those in which the negroes have increased more rapidly than in the country at large.

It is seen at once that the areas in which the negroes have decreased are mainly comprised in the northern of these states, principally in Delaware, Maryland, Virginia, Kentucky, and Missouri, and secondarily in Tennessee and North Carolina. There are also areas of decrease in Texas and small areas in the other states, but these are of little importance in comparison with the great areas of the border states in which the number of negroes has actually diminished.

On the other hand, the areas in which the negroes have increased more rapidly than in the country at large are found mainly in the southern parts of South Carolina, Georgia, Alabama, Mississippi, and eastern Texas, with nearly all of Arkansas and Florida. In other words, the most rapid increase of the race has been in the southern and western parts of the region under consideration. There does not appear to be any decided movement into the "Black Belt," which traverses the central part of South Carolina, Georgia, Alabama, and Mississippi. Indeed, the heaviest increase is south of this region.

PLATE VI.

LEGEND

Decrease

Increase less than the average of
the country.

Increase greater than the average
of the country.

The
Internet Archive
Birney Collection
Digitisation Project

Notice to
OCA Camera
Operator

☐ Foldout

page_____

☐ Missing Page

page_____

☐ Photocopy

page_____

☐ Brittle/Discolored
Paper

page_____

☐ Other problem:

Specify: _____

page_____

Specify: _____

page_____

Specify: _____

page_____

CONJUGAL CONDITION.

The conjugal condition of the negroes is set forth for the first time in the reports of the Eleventh Census. With the exception of the matter of divorce, it is summarized in the following diagram (Plate VII). This shows the proportion of males and females at various ages who were single, married or widowed. It shows that under the age of 15 there are practically no marriages among the race. Between 15 and 20 a small proportion, perhaps about one per cent., of males were married and 14 per cent. of the females. At ages between 20 and 25 a third of the males and nearly three-fifths of the females were married, and with advancing age a constantly increasing proportion of both sexes is either married or widowed. It is evident, however, that the women marry much younger than men. The proportion of widowed first becomes appreciable between the ages of 20 and 25 years. It increases much more rapidly among females than among males, and altogether the proportion of widows is many times greater than that of widowers, showing that many more widowers remarry than widows, and that they marry largely unmarried women.

Comparison of conjugal statistics of the negroes with those of the whites develops two points of difference. First, that the negroes marry younger than the whites; second, that the proportion of widows at most ages is greater than among whites. The first of these facts is in accord with the shorter life-period of the race; the second is a result of the greater death-rate of the race.

Statistics of divorce show more frequent severance of conjugal relations among the negroes than among the whites. The proportion of divorced persons to married persons in the United States at large among the native whites was 0.59 of 1 per cent., while among the negroes it was 0.67 of 1 per cent.

MORTALITY.

There is no question but that the rate of mortality among the negro population is considerably greater than among the

whites. It is not easy, however, to obtain an accurate measure
of the relative death-rates of the two races. The census
statistics upon this subject are unreliable, since the returns
from which they are derived are by no means complete.
Were the omissions uniformly distributed between the two
races, we might still derive a comparison from them regarding the death-rates of the two races, but unfortunately there
is every probability that the omissions are much greater pro-
portionally among the negroes than among the whites. It is
only in a few large southern cities which maintain a regis-
tration of deaths that reliable figures are to be had. In
these cities the relative death-rates during the census year
(1890) are shown in the following table:

	Total Population.	Native Whites.	Negroes.
St. Louis	19	17	35
Baltimore	25	22	36
New Orleans	28	22	37
Washington	26	19	38
Louisville	22	18	32

From these figures it appears that in the large cities the
annual death-rate of the negroes is very nearly if not quite
double that of the native whites. It is probable that in the
rural districts the disproportion among the death-rates is not
as great, since it is probable that a rural environment is better
suited to the negroes than the environment of a large city.
However this may be, there is no reasonable question, as
stated above, that the death-rate of the negroes is much
larger than that of the whites.

CRIMINALITY.

The proportion of criminals among the negroes is much
greater than among the whites. The statistics of the last
census show that the white prisoners of native extraction
confined in jails at the time the census was taken were in the
proportion of 9 to each 10,000 of all whites of native extraction, while the negro prisoners were in the proportion of 33

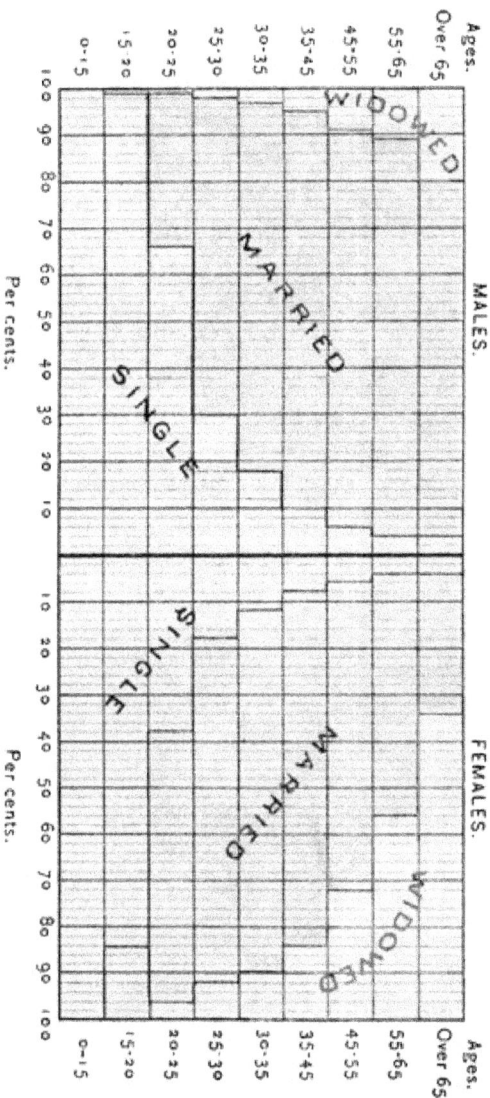

CONJUGAL CONDITION OF THE NEGRO ELEMENT.

MALES.

FEMALES.

Ages.

Over 65
55-65
45-55
35-45
30-35
25-30
20-25
15-20
0-15

WIDOWED

MARRIED

SINGLE

SINGLE

MARRIED

WIDOWED

Per cents.

Per cents.

Ages.

Over 65
55-65
45-55
35-45
30-35
25-30
20-25
15-20
0-15

PLATE VII.

to each 10,000 of the negro population. Thus it appears that the proportion of negroes was nearly four times as great as for the whites of native extraction. It should be added, however, that the commitments of negroes are for petty offenses in much greater proportion than among the whites.

PAUPERISM.

In respect to pauperism, the investigations of the census have been confined to paupers maintained in almshouses and have not been extended to those persons receiving outdoor relief, either permanent or temporary. The number of white paupers of native extraction in almshouses was found to be in the proportion of 8 to every 10,000 whites of native extraction, while the negro paupers were in the same proportion. Lest these figures should mislead, however, it must be added to this statement that in the south but little provision is made in the form of almshouses for the relief of the poor, this provision being confined almost entirely to the northern part of the country, a fact which in itself explains the small proportion of the negro paupers in almshouses. On the other hand, it is a matter of common knowledge to any resident of a southern city that the negroes form a disproportionately large element of the recipients of outdoor charity.

ILLITERACY AND EDUCATION.

Of the progress of the negro race in education, the statistics are by no means as full and comprehensive as is desirable. Such as we possess, however, go to indicate a remarkably rapid progress of the race in the elements of education. During the prevalence of slavery this race was kept in ignorance. Indeed, generally throughout the south it was held as a crime to teach the negroes to read and write, and naturally when they became freemen only a trifling proportion of them were acquainted with these elements of education. In 1870, five years after they became free, the records of the census show that only two-tenths of all the negroes over ten years of age in the country could write. Ten years later the proportion had increased to three-tenths of the whole number, and in 1890, only a generation after they were emancipated, not less than 43 out of every hundred negroes, of ten years of age and over, were able to read and write. These figures show a remarkably rapid progress in elementary education.

In 1860 the number of negroes who were enrolled in the schools of the south was absolutely trifling. Since the abolition of slavery the number has increased with the greatest rapidity. This is shown in the following table, which relates only to the inhabitants of the former slave states. The first column shows the proportion which the number of white children enrolled in the public schools bore to the white population, and the second column the proportion which the number of negro children in the public schools bore to the total negro population of these states.

	White.	Negro.
1870	13.50	3.07
1880	18.33	13.07
1890	21.92	18.71

It is seen from the above table that in 1870 the white pupils constituted 13.5 per cent. of the white population, and that in 20 years this proportion increased to nearly 22 per cent. On the other hand, the negro school children constituted in 1870 only 3 per cent. of all negroes, but that in 20 years it has increased to nearly 19 per cent. of all negroes. The proportion of negro school children increased at a far more rapid rate than that of the white school children, and in 1890 had nearly reached it.

The following table shows the proportion of school enrollment to population in 1890 in each of these states:

	Per Cent. of Enrollment to Population.	
	White.	Negro.
Delaware	19.12	16.38
Maryland	17.93	16.69
District of Columbia	15.24	17.61
Virginia	21.59	19.20
West Virginia	25.58	20.04
North Carolina	19.79	20.80
South Carolina	19.49	16.46
Georgia	21.40	15.51
Florida	24.37	21.85
Kentucky	22.27	20.40
Tennessee	26.49	23.58
Alabama	22.40	17.10
Mississippi	27.71	24.60
Louisiana	13.43	8.82
Texas	21.06	22.21
Arkansas	19.98	19.22
Missouri	23.24	21.76

An examination of this table shows that in the District of Columbia, North Carolina, and Texas the proportional enrollment of negroes was greater than that of the whites, while in the other states it was less.

The following table shows the rate of increase in the enrollment in each of these states from 1880 to 1890 :

	Per Cent.	
	White.	Negro.
Delaware	10.75	108.42
Maryland	20.07	35.78
District of Columbia	27.62	67.34
Virginia	44.44	78.77
West Virginia	33.68	59.72
North Carolina	29.51	22.97
South Carolina	45.64	55.33
Georgia	39.09	53.81
Florida	98.07	132.71
Kentucky	34.44	89.20
Tennessee	53.88	65.56
Alabama	66.95	53.52
Mississippi	30.75	50.66
Louisiana	61.72	42.56
Texas	179.36	143.65
Arkansas	101.08	121.29
Missouri	27.18	36.42

From this table it appears that in all excepting four states, namely, North Carolina, Alabama, Louisiana, and Texas, the enrollment of negro children in the public schools has increased more rapidly than has that of the whites.

Summing up this article in a paragraph, the following conclusions may be stated:

The negroes, while increasing rapidly in this country, are diminishing in numbers relative to the whites.

They are moving southward from the border states into those of the south Atlantic and the Gulf.

They prefer rural life rather than urban life.

The proportion of criminals among the negroes is much greater than among the whites, and that of paupers is at least as great.

In the matter of education, the number of negro attendants at school is far behind the number of whites, but is gaining rapidly upon that race.

Only one generation has elapsed since the slaves were freed. To raise a people from slavery to civilization is a matter, not of years, but of many generations. The progress which the race has made in this generation in industry, morality, and education is a source of the highest gratification to all friends of the race, to all excepting those who expected a miraculous conversion.

www.ingramcontent.com/pod-product-compliance
Lightning Source LLC
Chambersburg PA
CBHW021523270326
41930CB00008B/1058